This or That Pets

Is a FISH or a BIRD the Pet for Me?

by Jaclyn Jaycox

PEBBLE
a capstone imprint

Published by Pebble, an imprint of Capstone
1710 Roe Crest Drive, North Mankato, Minnesota 56003
capstonepub.com

Library of Congress Cataloging-in-Publication Data is available on the Library of Congress website.
ISBN: 9780756578954 (hardcover)
ISBN: 9780756578909 (paperback)
ISBN: 9780756578916 (ebook PDF)

Summary: Colorful feathers. Shiny scales. Fish and birds make very different pets! Compare these two eye-catching pets side by side. Which one costs more? Which pet lives longer? Is it easier to clean a bird cage or a fish aquarium? Learn the answers to these questions and more. Then decide which one might make the best pet for you!

Image Credits
Capstone Studio: Karon Dubke, 6, 9; Getty Images: BraunS, 15, Gins Wang, 18, vgajic, 12; Shutterstock: Africa Studio, 7, BestPhotoStudio, 5, Dzmitry Sarmont, 17, Ermolaev Alexander, 10, Media Home, 14, Natasha Pankina, background (throughout), panpilai paipa, Cover (top), Pixel-Shot, 16, 21, Praisaeng, 19, Solarisys, 11, Tomsickova Tatyana, 4, TY Lim, Cover (bottom), victoras, 13, Yaroslava, 20

Editorial Credits
Editor: Carrie Sheely; Designer: Bobbie Nuytten; Media Researcher: Jo Miller; Production Specialist: Whitney Schaefer

Printed and bound in China. PO 5834

Table of Contents

Getting a New Pet.................................4

Equipment 6

Food...8

Quiet or Noisy 10

Clean or Messy 12

Cheap or Costly............................. 14

Strong Bonds or Not...................... 16

Short or Long Lives 18

Which Pet Is Best for You?................. 20

Glossary 22

Read More 23

Internet Sites 23

Index....................................... 24

About the Author..................... 24

Words in **bold** are in the glossary.

Getting a New Pet

Squawk! Swish! Both birds and fish can be great pets! No pets are easy. They all need good care. But birds and fish easily fit into many families. Let's find out which pet might be better for you!

Equipment

Pet fish live in a tank called an **aquarium**. What tank size do you need? It depends on the fish size and how many you have. As a fish grows, it needs more room. Rocks, gravel, and plants go in the tank's bottom. A filter helps keep the water clean.

Birds need a bird cage. The cage size needed depends on the bird's size. A big cage gives birds more space to move. A liner, such as newspaper, goes in the bottom. Birds need a **perch** to stand on. They should have toys too.

Food

Fish eat flake food or pellets. Many fish also eat small pieces of vegetables. Some fish eat only plants. Others eat plants and meat.

Pet birds can eat different things. You can buy pellets from a pet store. Birds can eat some vegetables and fruits. Some birds can eat eggs and chicken.

Quiet or Noisy

Fish are very quiet as they swim. But birds can be noisy! They chirp and squawk. They whistle and chatter. Owners can teach some parrots and parakeets to talk.

Clean or Messy

Fish tanks should be cleaned at least every month. At least half of the water should be replaced. **Algae** needs to be scrubbed off the glass. Gravel needs to be cleaned too.

Birds can be very messy! They might toss around food. They can make messes outside of their cages. Bird cage liners should be changed every day. Food and water bowls need daily cleaning. Cages also need regular scrubbing.

Cheap or Costly

Many fish are fairly cheap to buy. But some **exotic** fish can be **expensive**. Some kinds of angelfish can cost hundreds of dollars. Most costs for fish will come at the beginning.

Some birds are more expensive than others. A parakeet might cost about $50. But some parrots cost thousands of dollars. Birds tend to cost more to care for than fish. Birds may need **veterinarian** visits. Most veterinarians do not treat fish.

Strong Bonds or Not

If you want a cuddly pet, a fish may not be for you. Fish stay in their tank. But they can be **social** animals. Some kinds of fish do well living in pairs or **schools**.

Many birds show **affection**. They may form strong bonds with their owners. Training and talking to your bird can strengthen the bond with your pet.

Short or Long Lives

When you get a pet, it becomes part of your family. You need to care for your pet throughout its life.

The life span of a bird or fish depends on the type. Some birds live around five years. Others can live more than 30 years. Many kinds of fish live three to five years. Some can live more than 10 years.

Which Pet Is Best for You?

Fish and birds make great pets. But they need different care. This activity can help you decide which one might be best for you.

What You Need:

- paper
- pen or pencil

What You Do:

1. On your paper, make two columns. Label one "bird" and the other "fish."

2. Ask yourself questions. How much time can you spend with a pet? Would you rather have a quiet pet or a noisy pet? Would you rather clean a fish tank or a bird cage? Be honest with your answers.

3. For each question, write a check mark in the column of the animal you chose.

4. At the end, the column with more check marks might be the pet for you!

Glossary

affection (uh-FEK-shuhn)—liking or caring for someone or something

algae (AL-jee)—small plants without roots or stems that grow in water

aquarium (uh-KWAYR-ee-uhm)—a place where people keep fish and other water animals

exotic (ig-ZAH-tik)—different or unusual

expensive (ik-SPEN-siv)—very costly

perch (PURCH)—a support, such as a stick or peg, on which a bird rests

school (SKOOL)—a large number of the same kind of fish swimming together

social (SOH-shuhl)—wanting to be near people or animals

veterinarian (vet-ur-uh-NER-ee-uhn)—a doctor trained to take care of animals

Read More

Klepeis, Alicia Z. *The History of Pet Birds*. Minneapolis: Pogo, 2024.

Klepeis, Alicia Z. *The History of Pet Fish*. Minneapolis: Pogo, 2024.

Rossiter, Brienna. *My Pet Fish*. Mendota Heights, MN: Little Blue House, 2022.

Internet Sites

Ducksters: Goldfish
ducksters.com/animals/goldfish.php

FunKids: Top 10 Facts About Fish!
funkidslive.com/learn/top-10-facts/top-10-facts-about-fish/

Kaytee: Best Pet Birds for Beginners
kaytee.com/learn-care/pet-birds/best-pet-birds-for-beginners

Index

affection, 17

bird training, 17

cage liners, 7
cages, 7, 13, 21
cleaning, 12, 13
costs, 14, 15

filters, 6
food, 8, 13

life spans, 19

noisiness, 10, 21

perches, 7, 22

schools, 16
socialness, 16

tank cleaning, 12
tanks, 6, 12, 16, 21
toys, 7
training, 17

About the Author

Jaclyn Jaycox is a children's book author and editor. When she's not writing, she loves reading and spending time with her family. She lives in southern Minnesota with her husband, two kids, and a spunky goldendoodle.